INTRODUCTION

Armies and civilizations have used biologic weapons for millennia. The increase of rogue nations, failing states, terrorists, and sub national actors since the close of the Cold War has highlighted the concern for mass casualty scenarios, both military and civilian, that would occur with a biologic weapon attack. The overriding lesson for our enemies is that successful challenges to the US must be indirect or asymmetrical. Ounce for ounce, the lethality of biologic agents is many times that of chemical or nuclear weapons.[1] Some currently feel that the threatened use of biologic weapons are our most pressing national interest. "Our gravest concern is closing the chilling gap between this new threat and our ability to respond to it."[2] Only in the last century has there been an attempt to control the use and development of biologic weapons. The United States significantly focused its attention on Weapons of Mass Destruction, and specifically biologic agents, after the Aum Shinrikyo cult released sarin gas in the subways of Japan, injuring thousands. The recent attack on the World Trade Center and the poor response to anthrax attacks via the US Postal Service have highlighted the need for a comprehensive policy dealing with all weapons of mass destruction, and specifically with biologic weapons. This paper will lay out the background of the development and uses of biologic weapons, investigate the current US strategy in dealing with bioterrorism, and develop options for improvement in our national defense.

DEFINITION

The US Government definition of bioterrorism is "the threat or intentional release of biologic agents for the purpose of influencing the conduct of government, or intimidating or coercing a civilian population."[3] A broader definition must be used for a complete analysis of this topic. "Bioterrorism is the intentional use of any microorganism, virus, infectious substance, or biological product that may be engineered as a result of biotechnology, or any naturally occurring or bioengineered component of any such microorganism, virus, infectious substance, or biologic product, to cause death, disease, or other biological malfunction in a human, an animal, a plant, or another living organism in order to influence the conduct of government or to intimidate or coerce a civilian population."[4] This definition accurately defines the problem. This definition more appropriately describes the ends, ways, and means that must be addressed for an accurate understanding of the current situation. While the majority of the literature written on this topic deals specifically with bioterrorism in terms of attacks on the people, two other significant targets must be included in an overall strategy. These are bioterrorism focused on agricultural targets and those focused on the nation's livestock. When you consider that agriculture accounts for approximately 1/6th of the entire US Gross Domestic Product, the impact of agricultural terrorism becomes extremely significant. Infecting or destroying either vegetable or meat products in the US will have significant impact on domestic and international policy.

There are several different classifications of what organisms are significant threats. Unfortunately, there is not universal agreement amongst various agencies or departments. The most consistent definition of organisms comes from the Centers of Disease Control and Prevention, which states that "high priority agents include organisms that pose a risk to national security because they: can be easily disseminated from person to person, cause high mortality, with potential for major public health impact, might cause panic and social disruption, and require special action for public health preparedness." These organisms include smallpox, anthrax, plague, botulinum toxin, tularemia, Ebola and Marburg virus, and Lassa and Junin virus. However, this list focuses solely on human-to-human spread or protection. A separate list of organisms that could potentially infect our food sources includes the above, plus viruses that cause foot and mouth disease, fungi, protozoa, as well as insects and weeds that may have been genetically altered to infect or destroy crops and animals.[5]

Unfortunately, the data from several databases that collate and analyze bioweapon attacks do not support the use of these agents as the highest threat agents.[6] Organisms such as shigella, salmonella, cholera, yersinia, and HIV have been used much more commonly. There are several reasons for this. These organisms, for the most part, occur in nature fairly freely, are easy to culture, store, and reproduce. They are all fairly hardy as well, and can withstand variations in temperature and oxygen for short periods of time.

THE CHANGING FACE OF TERRORISM

There is a significant amount of literature that has been written recently on the changing face of terrorism. This topic is important to understand so that clear decisions can be made concerning the threat and risk of biologic agents being used against the United States.

The most commonly espoused current theory on terrorism is that of catastrophic terrorism. These new terrorists do not have a purely political agenda, but are more bent on spreading a religious philosophy. These terrorists are a significant ideological change from the past, in that the recent terrorists who answer to their own deity are among the most lethal and difficult to deter.[7] The intrinsic shock value associated with the use or potential use of biologic weapons furthers their agenda. They are not just looking to make a statement, but are rather focused on mass destruction and mass casualties. The ready willingness of these persons to accept martyrdom for their actions makes current deterrence policies ineffective. Couple this with the fact that conventional bombings and threats may not be psychologically working to gain the effect these groups want due to oversaturation of the media makes the current terrorists and their ideals almost impossible to deter or counter under our current system.[8]

HISTORICAL BACKGROUND

The use of biologic weapons is well documented. Since 1900 there are 269 cases of bioterrorism identified in the open literature. In only 5 of these were actual biologic agents used in a mass casualty scenario. Only one of these attacks was successful. In 1986, the Rajneeshees used salmonella bacteria in a salad bar in Oregon, poisoning over 750, and causing 54 to be hospitalized.[9] Two other significant bioterrorism events in the US are important to mention. In the late 1990's, Larry Wayne Harris, a leader of the Aryan Nation, was arrested on several occasions for his possession, attempt to acquire or threaten to acquire several different biologic agents, most specifically Y. pestis, the organism responsible for plague. The fact that he was able to acquire this culture from a laboratory in the US sent shock waves throughout the US on the ease of acquiring these agents for destructive use. The other event occurred in the 1970's. Two ecologically driven men actually developed cultures for the organisms that cause bacterial meningitis, typhoid, and dysentery. They had also started vaccinating members of their cult against these organisms until they were caught. These two were able to gain access to hospital laboratories and acquire cultures of these bacteria with ease.

Ancient civilizations used dead bodies as biologic weapons. These warring factions would put corpses who died from contagious diseases into wells, contaminating the drinking water. Some feel that the plague that spread throughout Europe in the Middle Ages was worsened by the catapulting of dead bodies over besieged walls of cities, thereby infecting large, otherwise protected communities. Just prior to the Revolutionary War, Jeffrey Amherst advocated the use of the biologic agent smallpox, advising one of his subordinates "you will do well to try to [infect] the Indians by means of blankets as well as to try every other method that can serve to extirpate this execrable race."[10]

During World War I, both the Germans and the French succeeded in infecting livestock with anthrax and glanders, which was then spread to the troops as well as other animals. In the 1920's in Japan, huge facilities for the development and testing of various biologic weapons were developed. Testing included giving anthrax laced chocolate bars to children, the development of bombs laden with plague-infected fleas, and investigations into gas gangrene.[11]

The highly publicized mailing of anthrax letters to several members of Congress and to a media outlet, infecting 22 people in late 2001 is the most recent example. Buildings were evacuated for weeks, and three are still closed today. Twenty-two people were diagnosed with either inhalational or topical anthrax, and five died. Mail workers, postal employees, congressional aides and staffers were all screened, treated with antibiotics or offered the anthrax vaccine. Over 40,000 people took antibiotics from this exposure. The public health labs were completely overloaded with mail, air, and particle samples to test and evaluate. The media coverage was continuous, and was often filled with incorrect or sensationalist information. Jurisdictional issue over who investigates, collects data, and who can release data to whom became a significant glaring error in this episode of bioterrorism. Mail was radiated and rerouted from some of the busiest hubs of mail processing, and the effects are still being realized today. The overall public reaction was totally out of control with respect to the level of threat.[12]

The last major outbreak of smallpox occurred in India in 1973-4. Hundreds of healthcare workers and epidemiologists were sent from around the world to eradicate the spread. Significant quarantine issues and extensive nomadic tracking was required to finally contain this outbreak. Religious and ethnic clashes had to be overcome to effectively eradicate the disease. This lasted over a year, and required tremendous worldwide expenditures and support from international health organizations.[13]

Since World War II, the development and research into offensive biologic weapons has increased exponentially, with the development and subsequent disbandment of the huge Biopreparat in USSR and US investigations until 1972 into offensive weapons capabilities. Currently, biologic weapons are suspected to be in use or development in Iraq, Iran, Syria, China, South Africa, North Korea, Russia, Israel, Taiwan, Cuba, Sudan, India, Pakistan, and Kazakhstan.[14]

TREATIES AND CONVENTIONS

The initial control over the use of biologic weapons was established during the Hague

Conventions of 1899 and 1907. The first global attempt at eliminating biologic weapons was the Geneva Convention of 1925. This document, in its declaration, prohibited the use of biologic weapons. It did not prohibit the development, research, or production of these weapons. This Convention applied only to the signatories of the document, and had no provisions for testing or verification.

A further attempt at the control and use of these weapons is the one that is currently in place. The Biologic Weapons Convention was developed in 1972, with full implementation in 1975. There are now over 160 signatories to this convention, which is intended to control the proliferation, development and use of biologic weapons. There have been four revisions of this convention since 1972, the last occurring in 1991. This treaty has many significant drawbacks. These drawbacks include the fact that there is no definition of legal vs. Illegal research, the fact that there are no non-compliance threats built into the document, and there is no oversight committee currently in place to certify or verify this treaty. The US is not a signatory to this convention because we feel it is not a strong enough document, and will allow our adversaries critical information on defenses and preparation capabilities. It is based on a traditional arms control treaty format, which does not work in unconventional dual use warfare control. The US feels this treaty will significantly compromise national security because of the release of classified information required. The US also feels that our adversaries could use this treaty to skirt and bypass the requirements in this treaty.[15] Also, non-signatories such as Israel, Syria, Morocco, and Algeria cannot be inspected or held to the provisions of this convention.[16]

The Australia Group has also been established to control the delivery of "dual use" technology to states with an interest in controlling the spread of WMD development. It, like the other treaties, does not carry significant enforcement or regulatory policies, especially when dealing with non-state or sub-state actors.[17]

The major problems with these treaties is that detecting violations is nearly impossible, unless self-reported. These treaties only apply to sovereign nation-states, and do not deal with terrorist organizations or individuals who develop or use biologic weapons.

HOW TO EVALUATE THE THREAT

Before we establish a nationwide policy dealing with bioterrorism, we must first define what constitutes this threat. This paper proposes four questions to identify and measure the level of the threat of bioterrorism. The first question to answer is: Are there significant states or actors who have interest in bioweapons research and development? The current answer is yes. The record and interest in bioweapons are significant. The US was actively involved in offensive bioweaponry until 1972. The anthrax outbreak near a bioweapons facility in Russia in 1979 removed any doubt of the Russians developing offensive biologic weapons. There is significant evidence that China, Egypt, India, Iran, Iraq, Israel, Libya, North Korea, Pakistan, Russia, Syria, South Africa and Taiwan are currently developing offensive bioweaponry or possess sufficient civilian capability to do so. Of these, Iran, Iraq, Libya, North Korea, and Syria are listed as states that sponsor terrorism.[18] Also, the difficulty in identifying and tracking covert bioweapon research and development masks who is actually developing the technology necessary to deliver biologic agents.

The second question is: Does the country/actor have the ability to weaponize or deliver biologic agents? The current answer is unknown, and this poses significant difficulties in analyzing the threat. There are many countries, as stated above, that have significant bioweapons programs, yet to date there has never been a confirmed attack using biologic weapons. The ability to store, transmit and disseminate these agents via conventional means poses a significant problem for all researchers. The researchers have yet to solve the problem of heat and oxygen stability with these agents. Dissemination via conventional munitions would not cause the catastrophic level of disease outbreak or death that many pursue. However, with the rapidly expanding field of biotechnology, it may be easy over the next decade to counter these obstacles with gene manipulation and organism protection methods.

The third question we must answer is: Can we effectively control and counter bioweapons and their precursors? The current answer is no. There are effective vaccines, antibiotics, physical barriers, and plenty of research and development opportunities to help combat bioweaponry. The quantities of these vaccines are minimal and the cost for development and storage are prohibitive. Several are only in research and development phases at present and are not readily available to the public or first responders. Nor are these vaccines moneymakers for pharmaceutical companies, so the priority for research and development are low. Also, the US cannot currently effectively control dual use products that states or actors can acquire with relative ease and convert into a bioweapons laboratory.

The final question to consider is: Will state/actors use bioweapons? This is the most difficult question to answer. Some experts feel that bioweapons are unnecessary because terrorists are just as successful now using traditional weaponry, which is much easier to obtain, deliver, and escape the effects of. Added to this is the fact that no state or actor has used these agents as an act of terrorism for mass casualties since the early 1700's. However, there are others who feel that the possession of biologic weapons is necessary for asymmetric warfare, and the theory of catastrophic terrorism will require their use once obtained.

RISK ASSESSMENT

There are three competing theories in use today to describe the risk of bioterrorism against the US. These theories answer the four questions above differently in developing a potential national strategy.

The first theory assures an attack in the near future. This theory defines current US strategy.

"…the threat is real, growing, extremely dangerous, and growing rapidly."

"…there is no margin for error, and no chance to learn from one's mistakes."[19]

"Within the next 10 years, there was a 100% chance of a chemical or biological attack in our country."[20]

"US must raise bioterrorism to the top of the national agenda."[21]

This theory believes that the current actors possess the required precursors, have the ability to deliver the agents, have the desire to use the agents, and that we cannot currently combat the threat. Several factors point towards the use of biologic weapons in the near future. First is the fact that non-state actors may be harbored in rogue states and given state level resources. Future advances in genetics and engineering will decrease the technologic know-how. Finally, our public health and medical infrastructure has been shown to be incapable of dealing with mass casualty situations.[22] With this information being publicly shared almost daily in news broadcasts and media, our adversaries are sure to pick up on these vulnerabilities.

The National Strategy for Homeland Security states that biologic weapons are relatively easy to produce, require straightforward technical skills and basic equipment, and a small seed stock. The effects of these agents will be delayed, so rapid detection must be a key.

The proponents see a rapid expansion of current technology, a brain drain from the former Soviet Republic, and the requirement by ideological terrorists to inflict mass casualties as markers for an assured attack. They feel that the technology is rather straightforward, and the capabilities for acquisition, development, and dissemination are within the grasp of terrorists. Also, some feel that the effects of current conventional bombs and killings are not psychologically effective anymore, and more must be used to inflict the desired effect. This is obviously the most, and some would say prohibitively, expensive theory to adopt.

The second theory is that these weapons, while attractive, are too costly to develop, too difficult to employ in terms of technology and resources, and are too unpredictable. These theorists would answer the above questions as such: While there may be some interest in developing biologic weapons, the means to accurately deliver them without infecting my own population is not available, and I have other means to enact my beliefs. These proponents use the Aum Shinrikyo cult in Japan as an example. They were financed with billions of dollars and had several key technicians skilled in biotechnology, but could never demonstrate effective use of either botulinum toxin or anthrax.[23] Funding of this would not significantly impact the US. The major problem with this theory is that this will only worsen the unpreparedness of the US for bioterrorism attacks. Ignoring the results of many national sponsored training events and the anthrax exposure shortcomings will only lead to a more catastrophic result in the future.

An alternate theory is the one most espoused by bioterror experts. The proponents of this theory state that there is current active research on the use of offensive bioweapons, but there use and delivery is not currently capable of causing mass casualties, and that the US can effectively counter the threat with active research and development and preparedness. President Bush, in the current National Strategy for Homeland Security, stated, "we have to accept some level of terrorist risk as a permanent condition."[24] A current General Accounting Office (GAO) report states that there is a low probability of a domestic biowarfare attack.[25] This theory relates a low probability of occurrence. However, the threat is significant and only with proper management and resources can we reduce the threat of a catastrophic outcome. They describe the threat requires both significant attention and resources, but should be weighed against all of the other Chemical, Biologic, Radiation, Nuclear, and high Energy (CBRNE) threats. The most significant problem with this theory is that there are no guidelines on how to size the threat or responses.[26]

CURRENT POLICY

Currently, the president has declared that the nations first priority is to prevent terrorist attacks against critical structures. We must be able to detect the enemy before they strike, prevent them from entering our country, and eliminate the threat to our homeland.[27] Critical structures for the United States are defined in the National Strategy for Homeland Security. They include agriculture, food, water, public health, emergency services, government offices, defense industrial bases, information's and telecommunications, energy, transportation, banking and finance, chemical, postal and shipping. All must be protected against terrorist threats.[28] This is too broad of a list to effectively prioritize, as it includes a large proportion of all workplaces, buildings, and infrastructure. However, the US does not have a comprehensive policy dealing either with WMD or specifically with bioterrorism. What it currently uses is a conglomeration of laws, regulations, agency policies and agendas, and various funding initiatives to coordinate for bioterrorism defense.

There are over 20 different agencies who have some level of responsibility for bioterrorism defenses, including the Departments of Health and Human Services (HHS), Justice (DOJ), Energy, Veteran Affairs, Defense (DoD), Agriculture (USDA), Treasury, Transportation, the Environmental Protection Agency, Federal Emergency Management Agency (FEMA), General Services Administration, American Red Cross, US Postal Service and the Centers for Disease Control and Prevention (CDC). No less than five of these have different crisis response teams that are to deploy in case of a bioterrorist attack. The Federal Emergency Management Agency currently is the lead agent in charge of consequence management in CONUS. HHS has the responsibility to coordinate medical emergencies, improve surveillance, securing the National Pharmaceutical stockpile, and investment in medical research and development to prevent or minimize the effects of biologic agents.[29]

We have insufficient human intelligence with terrorist organizations, and it is unclear what to do with information received. We also cannot effectively attack the funding of theses terror organizations.[30] There is significant duplication of effort, and lack of a clear vision and focus under the current system. A GAO report released in 2001 reveals a fragmented coordination of federal terrorism research and preparedness, and a poor response program.[31]

There is limited accountability to any organization, and no unity of effort. Several different agencies have developed their own threat list of biowarfare agents, making training and research and development even more difficult. There is a lack of participation of hospitals and the private health community in training or mass casualty drills at regional levels. The current Public Health infrastructure is severely under-resourced. The current West Nile Virus outbreak has overtaxed the Public Health and laboratory systems in the US. There is little surge capability present in hospitals or emergency rooms throughout the United States. Finally, training of first responders throughout the United States is inadequate.[32]

9

While the threat against humans has had some effort, the current state of bioterrorism preparedness against foodstuffs and agriculture is essentially non-existent. The US Department of Agriculture cannot presently protect animal and plant foods.[33] If an attack occurred against an agriculture target, it could have devastating effects on the US, allies, and trade partners. The US unpreparedness can be compared to Europe's dealings with Mad Cow Disease. These effects are still being felt worldwide due to a lack of surveillance, diagnosis, and effective quarantine procedures.

Federal, state, and local public health officials are already stressed by other problems, and have not effectively planned for bioterrorism. The CDC has developed a strategic plan. This preparedness planning is a challenge, but the consequences of being unprepared are devastating. The focus must be on those agents that pose the greatest threat to US health and security. The CDC has developed their own list of agents; with class A being the most likely to cause significant death and illness. The CDC will provide guidelines, support, and technical assistance, and self-assessment tools to states and municipalities for bioterrorism preparedness.[34]

The US Government has attempted to fix these deficiencies. The FY 2003 Budget proposes in excess of 5.9 billion dollars to be spent on bioterrorism prevention. The Bioterrorism Preparedness Act and the National Public Health and Bioterrorism Readiness Act, both signed in 2001, call for significant increases in public health, intelligence gathering, response training, and funding. However, there is still no consolidated agency or department that is successfully managing the threat.[35]

There is currently a cooperative agreement between National Governor's Association, CDC, DOJ, and FEMA on how the US will respond to bioterrorism. Not having state plans or integrated plans is unacceptable. Many states are waiting for a national plan to enmesh their plan into, and this has led to a very haphazard and uneven implementation plan throughout the US.[36]

The recent Dark Winter Exercise held in 2000 sums up all of the shortcomings that exist in homeland bioterrorism defense. During the portion called exercise TOPOFF, a deliberate release of plague occurred in Denver. The city of Denver and the state of Colorado were unable to respond medically with enough surge capability. There were significant shortages in antibiotics, respirators, beds, and antibiotics within 48 hours of the start of the exercise. State and national quarantine issues were raised without resolution at senior levels. The ability to use the press and media as an information source was severely limited. The final determination was that the systems and resources now in place would be hard pressed to successfully manage a bioweapons attack.

"Large vulnerabilities in biowarfare defense posture remain." [37] In summary, we have made some progress, but success is a long way off. Science and technology needs to focus on vaccines, antibiotics, and early warning and identification technologies to protect the United States. We must develop a national strategy to what is an international problem.

HOW TO DETER?

The US has used deterrence theory with nuclear weapons for decades. Nuclear deterrence as was achieved through the policy of mutually assured deterrence will not work with bioterrorism. A new doctrine must be developed to deter the threat. This deterrence and dissuasion must focus on not only preventing the attack, but also preventing the acquisition of agents and technology. It must also focus on decreasing the likelihood that an attack will cause significant death and illness and disruption of the American way of life. Only then will deterrence be effective.

A new deterrence doctrine must develop the three following areas to impact the threat to be effective. The US must determine where are the opportunities for deterrence, what are the elements of deterrence, and what are the instruments of deterrence. All three of these need to be coordinated in a national plan.

There are many areas where the US can easily intervene to decrease the threat. These areas include denial of acquisition of biologic agents and their precursors, and intervening in delivery systems development and acquisition. Infiltrating these terrorist cells, organizations, and rogue state bioweapons research and development processes will be extremely difficult, if not impossible. Trying to change the ideology and motivation through information dominance and psychological operations on a worldwide scale, with multiple different groups and targets also poses insurmountable problems at present.

This new doctrine focuses on the following four elements of deterrence. These are identifying areas of intervention, cost/benefit manipulation, communication, and US resolve and national will. Identifying the action to be deterred must be coordinated at the national level. While this seems simple, the list of opportunities described above and the ability to influence these targets poses significant difficulties currently for the United States. The US must develop a clear priority of which actions and interventions will have the most benefit in a resource-constrained environment. The US must prioritize the elements of national power assigned to

11

each action they are attempting to deter.

Secondly, cost/benefit manipulation of the adversary is a critical element of deterrence theory. If the US can place the potential cost, not only in monetary terms, but resources and personnel, above the potential benefits, we can effectively deter. This must get into the funding, as well as the mindset of our adversaries to be effective. Third, the US must be able to clearly communicate this strategy to our potential adversaries threats. Finally, we must appear credible and unwavering in achieving our goal.

There are several instruments of deterrence the US must impact to be effective in the war on bioterror. Communication is key, as stated above. The US must have a clear, concise, predictable message on terror. This must be transmitted publicly, and be credible and understandable to all potential adversaries.

Identifying and predicting possible agents to be used, as well as targets of opportunity the enemy will try to exploit against the US, are key to future information operations. These actions will guide the US development of active and passive protection plans against people, facilities, and agribusiness. These may include animal, human, and plant vaccines, antibiotic depots, and possible gene manipulation of crops and animals to prevent the effects of these agents. This deterrence doctrine must include a better definition of infrastructure priorities, and effective means to protect them.

The US must have effective denial and defensive postures in place. We must make it too hard for the enemy to develop these biologic agents and employ them through dual use enforcement, strengthening treaties and cooperative agreements, reducing anonymity of actors, and stricter control of laboratory specimens and technologies.

If employed, the US must reduce the impact of these biologic agents. Effective consequence management, public health infrastructure, rapid identification, antibiotics, effective and timely decontamination, sufficient lab capabilities and evacuation procedures must be developed.

Finally, the US must have an effective and credible punitive arm to fully combat the war on terror. This includes not just the military, but also all elements of national power. The US must use the full range of diplomatic, monetary and information operations to discredit and unmask bioterrorists, and assure swift punishment for breaches of trust and security.[38]

RECOMMENDATIONS

First and foremost, we must understand that this is a worldwide threat. No single nation can effectively implement and effect this global problem. As the world's only superpower, the United States must take the lead in internal protection, as well as leading the drive to rid the world of these weapons and the people and organizations that are determined to use them.

The United States must coordinate bioterrorism preparedness at one central department. An Office of Bioterrorism Preparedness (OBP) would serve as the focal point for all plans and policies on bioterrorism preparedness. This must be an Office within the Department of Homeland Defense. This Office should have representatives from the following agencies assigned on a permanent basis: Department of Defense, Department of Agriculture, Environmental Protection Agency, Department of Health and Human Services, Federal Emergency Response Agency, and American Red Cross. Other departments and agencies should have access to this Office and be able to provide timely information and resources, including the Department of Justice, Department of Interior, and Department of Energy. The US goal must be to create an environment with few actors and limited capabilities. This will be achieved through military preparedness, intelligence, counterterrorism, cooperative threat reduction, diplomacy, export controls, and the use of force if necessary.

This central organization must develop an annual preparedness report for the US, in conjunction with the National Security Strategy. It must coordinate and prepare bioweapons threat assessments throughout the various agencies. It must supervise all plans and policies dealing with bioterrorism.

This Office will be responsible for centralized funding of all aspects of bioterrorism defense and deterrence. Coordinating funding for all plans, projects, exercises, response teams must be developed at the national level. Priorities must be established for funding for bioterrorism research and development, with specific agencies earmarked for their accountability. Priorities need to be set for the research and development of vaccines, antimicrobials, and antidotes. This needs to be closely tied with the civilian marketplace and the pharmaceutical industry to prevent duplication of effort and to set priorities for the US. This will decrease the amount of duplication of effort in the various departments presently, and allow a unity of focus under the director of Homeland Security.

Intelligence gathering on bioweapons must be centralized. The lead for this should be the Department of Justice section within the OBP. In coordination with the CIA, FBI, and other intelligence agencies, this Office must analyze and develop strategies for dealing with various biowarfare agents. Currently, early warning is extremely hard to do. With a central repository of information from all departments, a better threat assessment and early warning can be gained in a timely fashion. The US needs to reinvest in human intelligence as well. Getting inside of these organizations and terrorist states may be the only way to effectively gather critical information in a timely fashion. It is obvious that the current dependence on electronic and signal intelligence is not sufficient for today's threat.

Incident management planning must be initiated at the national level, with clearly defined roles and responsibilities for all departments, states and local municipalities. FEMA should retain the lead in this area, with close ties for on scene control with the Department of Justice. Once this is accomplished, states and municipalities can better plan for their own response, identify what is lacking in the community, and allocate resources. The US must develop matrices for state and local agencies to integrate into a seamless response system. Hasty and deliberate decontamination of sites and buildings needs to be a part of national disaster response.

This Office must be responsible for developing a standard training program for first responders and health care providers on the possible threat agents. The agents used in bioweaponry cause diseases that are not routinely seen by first responders or primary care physicians.[39] Without adequate training, the time from infection to diagnosis will be too long for effective control of the disease outbreak and effective prophylaxis. This training program must then be de-centralized, allowing states and municipalities to train their resources accordingly. The input from DoD, FEMA, and HHS will be critical in developing the appropriate standards and guidelines. The Department of Health and Human Services, through the CDC, should be the lead agent for training programs for first responders.

Too much money and effort have been spent on centralized emergency response teams for the United States. These have been shown to be ineffective and untimely. The focus for training resources and funding needs to be on the first responders and medical assets within the community and state. Inefficient teams that may take days to respond are a waste of the nation's limited resources. These teams need to be disbanded, and the operational and maintenance funds turned back to this Office for other uses.

Public Health preparedness needs to be a primary focus for this Office. This portion of bioterrorism preparedness should also have HHS as the lead agent. Public Health officials must become part of the National Security team.[40] There are four areas of focus for this Office with respect to Public Health preparedness. The first is coordinating a medical and public health response plan, which must include OEP, FEMA, DOD/VA, as well as private sector hospitals and health care organizations. Second, they must improve surveillance in local and regional laboratories, to include detecting organisms, which may be used in bioterrorism. They have to coordinate a rapid response for the National Pharmaceutical Stockpile to locations and regions. Finally, there has to be a focus on prevention, as mandated by the Antiterrorism and Effective Death Penalty Act of 1996. This mandated the CDC track and regulates the sale and transfer of certain biologic agents.[41]

The first step in preparedness is detection. The epidemiologists at state and local level must have the expertise and resources to rapidly and correctly identify biologic agents. Early detection is critical, and requires improved communications systems in the public health arena. To this end the CDC is developing local partnerships with multilevel laboratory response network in case of a suspected attack. This network will supply the appropriate detection agents, as well as developing and testing an on-line database for transmission of critical medical information.

The second step involves appropriate emergency response. The current stockpile developed (National Pharmaceutical Stockpile) of appropriate vaccines and drugs needs to be immediately available throughout the nation. This stockpile must include agents against agricultural targets as well. There must also be a significant increase in research and development on effective drugs and vaccines for both human and animal targets. Medical treatment and prophylaxis needs to start as early as possible. This is only possible with trained, experienced epidemiologists at state and local level promptly responding to early warnings identified by first responders and physicians. Finally, an environmental decontamination plan needs to be developed.

The third step is to develop an effective communications plan. Local media, Internet resources, and national information systems need to be developed. [42] These plans must include methods to inform public and media outlets on bioterrorism, threats, and safety measures.[43]

The final step is to realistically look at issues of isolation and quarantining families, cities, states, and countries.[44] All of the exercises have identified that this issue is one of the most difficult to plan for or execute. However, to prevent the spread of either human or agricultural diseases and worsen the event, a critical evaluation on how to effectively quarantine must be incorporated into a national plan.

This Office must develop a counterproliferation plan. Several sections, including Justice, Interior, and INS will all have significant input into the development of an effective plan. They must develop a list of restricted items for export control and local sales, to include possible dual use technologies, organisms, and laboratory capabilities that may be used in a covert program. This list must be updated frequently, and the results incorporated into the Australia Group.

Prevention must include preemption when necessary. Locating and destroying stockpiles of agents is critical. Destroying laboratories or production facilities is necessary to deter the threat. Putting significant military enforcement criteria into existing treaties and conventions must occur. Otherwise, the conventions will carry no weight, and the problems the UN is currently dealing with in Iraq on verification of Weapons of Mass Destruction laboratories will be commonplace throughout the world.

The US needs to better define and prioritize its critical structures. The current list is too long and large to effectively prioritize protective postures. Active and passive means of protecting, surveillance measures, and defending critical infrastructures must be developed. This must be done at the national level, but a large portion of this must fall on the private sector to protect their structures and personnel. The private sector needs to have better ties with the FBI and other information agencies to effectively plan for defense.

The US should also consider a way to provide peaceable research opportunities for the large number of unemployed Soviet scientists who were actively involved in biowarfare.[45] The private sector must be actively involved in this, as well as Department of Defense, Agriculture, and State. We should actively use their knowledge to effectively plan for defensive requirements in the US. Removing this source of knowledge from the marketplace for terrorists and rogue states will make it much more difficult for them to develop these weapons.

States have five clear missions to prepare for bioterrorism defense. The first is effective leadership. Emergency response needs to be pre-planned and coordinated at the state level. Community needs and resources need to be identified and prioritized at the state level. Training, from first responders to Emergency Operations Centers needs to be conducted and integrated. Finally, and most importantly, a definition of responsibilities and missions needs to be developed at the national level, and then integrated into states' plans. Surge capabilities for overwhelming number of patients must be dealt with at the local and state level. Alternative sites for patients, to include schools, armories, malls, or other large sites with power must be investigated and planned at the local level. Also, mortuary needs and waste control of contaminated and non-contaminated waste is a significant issue that states and municipalities must plan for.[46]

All of the above recommendations must include agricultural bioterrorism planning and prevention as well. Agriculture and agribusiness must be a critical infrastructure requiring effective protection and defense. The USDA must be included in developing all plans, policies, and research and development recommendations. FDA field food inspectors, as first responders, also need to be trained in diagnosing and early warning for agricultural terrorism. Veterinarians, farmers, and meat processing facilities must all be considered first responders with respect to agricultural bioterrorism. Quarantining foodstuffs and livestock will be especially difficult to enforce and regulate, unless properly planned for.

Wargaming is also essential, at all levels. This Office must develop local and regional exercises. These exercises must include all of the above listed agencies, plus private hospitals and organizations that are normally excluded or role-played. These exercises need to be run on a regular basis, proctored, with lessons learned archived and tracked to improve the nations' defense. [47]

Finally, in conjunction with the Department of State and Defense, a clear and credible policy must be developed with dealing with all rogue states, actors, and terrorists. Significant involvement with the United Nations, World Court, and other multinational organizations must eliminate safe harbors and funding for these adversaries. Effective means of cash flow curtailment must be implemented immediately to cut off the large quantities of money involved in terrorist organizations. This must be a worldwide effort. The US must take the lead in the development of a new Biologic Weapons Convention, and be an initial signatory to the process. This convention must include a serious implementation of the following items. First, strict terms on active and passive defense research and development must be written into the document. Active defense (retaliatory strikes in kind) should be severely limited, if not prohibited. A strong passive defense plan for vaccination and antibiotic research must be in place. Secondly, terms of routine and challenge inspections, with enforcement criteria for non-compliance, must be developed. There must be a way to protect vital national interest and private sector research when disclosing information to this convention. Finally, a standing agency must either be developed or included in another international organization for oversight and reporting. This could be through the UN Security Council or the World Court for reporting and enforcement.[48]

A word of caution must be inserted. A plan that is too aggressive will invade personal liberties and may be unworkable at the local level. The draft Model State Emergency Health Powers Act was proposed after the attacks on the World Trade Center. This Act would give unlimited power to the governor of a state to declare and control a disease outbreak with only subjective criteria. There are several groups, including AIDS activists, religious groups who do not

17

believe in vaccinations, and civil liberties groups, who believe this document would allow significant invasion into private health records and interfere with doctor-patient confidentiality. In the wrong hands, it could lead to the quarantining of people with AIDS, and have significant restrictions on travel and medical care. [49]

CONCLUSIONS

Bioterrorism is a threat the United States, and the entire world, must deal with resolutely, promptly, and effectively. There is significant historical precedent for the use of bioweapons. There are multiple sovereign states and terrorist cells dedicated on the proliferation of these weapons of mass destruction. Significant advances in biotechnology, and the globalization of these technologies will make it easier for all to develop and deliver these agents. A new terrorism mindset has developed increasing the likelihood of the use of weapons of mass destruction.

Currently the United States is ill prepared to protect its homeland against a significant attack. The US must develop a new doctrine of deterrence and dissuasion attacking all levels of bioweapons development, procurement, and use. This must be headed at the national level under the Department of Homeland Defense. Integration of the Office of Bioterrorism Preparedness with other agencies throughout the US Government must be undertaken immediately to prevent a mass casualty scenario in the future, disrupting and interfering with the freedoms we hold so dear. The US must be clear in its message, and hold steadfast to her resolve in preventing these attacks through adequate deterrence and preparedness as outlined above.

"Even without the threat of war, investment in a national defense ensures preparedness and acts as a deterrence against hostile acts."[50]

(Word count 7299)

ENDNOTES

[1] Frank J. Cilifullo, Sharon L. Cardash, and Gordon N Lederman, <u>Combating Chemical, Biological, Radiological and Nuclear Terrorism: A Comprehensive Strategy</u> (Washington, D.C.: Center for Strategic and International Studies, December 2000), 3.

[2] Peter Ross Range. "Preparing for Bioterrorism," <u>New Democrats Online</u> 15 November 2001 [journal on-line]; available from <http://www.ndol.org/ndol_ci.cfm?contentid=3924& kaid=124&subid=160>; Internet; accessed 21 September 2002.

[3] General Accounting Office, <u>Bioterrorism Federal Research and Preparedness Activities</u> (Washington, D.C.: US General Accounting Office, September 2001), 1.

[4] <u>The Model State Emergency Health Powers Act (Draft As of 23 October 2001)</u> (Washington, D.C.: Center for Law and the Public's Health at Georgetown and Johns Hopkins Universities, 2001) 9.

[5] These lists come from several sections from the following two articles: Centers for Disease Control and Prevention, " Biological and Chemical Terrorism: Strategic Plan for Preparedness and Response. Recommendations of the CDC Strategic Planning Workgroup" <u>Morbidity and Mortality Weekly Report</u> no. 49 RR-4(2000): 1-14. Henry S Parker, <u>Agricultural Bioterrorism: A Federal Strategy to Meet the Threat</u> (Washington, D.C.: Institute for National Strategic Studies, National Defense University,2002).

[6] W. Seth Carus, <u>Working Paper Bioterrorism and Biocrimes</u> (Washington, D.C.: Center For Counterproliferation Research, National Defense University, August 1998 (February 2001 Revision)) 6-20.

[7] This theory of terrorism is discussed in multiple references in this paper. The best discussion is in Brad Roberts and Michael Moodie, "Biologic Weapons: Toward a Threat Reduction Strategy." <u>Defense Horizons</u> 15 (July 2002): 1-8.

[8] This is further discussed in Cilifullo and Cardash, 4.

[9] Carus, 7.

[10] Anthony Daniels, "Germs Against Man." <u>National Review</u> 53 (December 3, 2001): 42-44.

[11] Ibid, 42-4.

[12] The results of the attacks on the US with anthrax are very well documented and explained in the following two citations. Kenneth Shine, "Bioterrorism From Panic to Preparedness." <u>RAND Review</u> (August 2002): [database on-line]; available at ProQuest; accessed 21 September 2002. Robert Strongin, <u>Bioterrorism: Summary of a CRS/National Health Policy Seminar on Federal, State, and Local Public Health Preparedness</u> (Washington, D.C.: Congressional Research Service, Library of Congress. 21 December 2001).

[13] James Cross Giblin, <u>When Plague Strikes: the Black Death, Smallpox, AIDS</u> (New York: HarperCollins, 1995), 107-8.

[14] Congress, Senate, Senate Armed Services Committee, Subcommittee on National Security, <u>Combating Terrorism: Federal Response to a Biologic Weapons Attack</u> 107th Cong., 1st sess, 23 July 2001, 4., and John R. Bolton, "The U.S. Position on the Biologic Weapons Convention: Combating the BW Threat." Speech delivered to the U.S. Embassy Tokyo 27 August 2002; available from <http://usembassy.state.gov/tokyo/wwwhse1631.html>; Internet; accessed 21 September 2002.

[15] Bolton, 2-3.

[16] An excellent discussion on the current state of the Biologic Weapons Convention and its drawbacks is found in Malcolm Dando, <u>Biologic Warfare in the 21st Century</u>, (New York: Brassey's, 1994), 65-85.

[17] Ibid, 4.

[18] Amy Smithson and Leslie Ann Levy, <u>Ataxia: The Chemical and Biological Terrorism Threat and US Response</u> (Washington, D.C.: The Henry L. Stimson Center, 1999), 46-7.

[19] Bolton, 2.

[20] As quoted in Frank J. Cilifullo, et al., <u>Defending America in the 21st Century New Challenges, New Organizations, and New Policies</u> (Washington, D.C.: Center For Strategic and International Studies, 2000), 2.

[21] Range, 1.

[22] Multiple references clearly denote the lack of US preparedness. See Cilifullo, <u>Combating Chemical, Biological, Radiological and Nuclear Terrorism: A Comprehensive Strategy</u>, 4, for further information.

[23] See an excellent discussion of the Aum Shinrikyo cult and their strategies in Smithson, chapter 3.

[24] George W. Bush, <u>National Strategy for Homeland Security</u> (Washington, D.C.: Office Of Homeland Security, July 2002), 2.

[25] General Accounting Office, 5.

[26] These theories are summarized from Center for Counterproliferation Research, <u>Chemical, Biological, Radiological, and Nuclear Terrorism: The Threat According to the Current Unclassified Literature</u> (Washington, D.C.: National Defense University, 31 May 2002), 8-11.

[27] <u>National Strategy for Homeland Security</u>, 2.

[28] Ibid, 29.

[29] Tommy Thompson, "Facing the Threat of Bioterrorism: Plans and Priorities for the Bush Administration." Speech given to the National Governors Association, 10 July 2001; available

from <http://www.hhs.gov/news/speech/2001/010710.html>; Internet; accessed 21 September 2002.

[30] National Strategy for Homeland Security, 25.

[31] GAO, 5-15.

[32] Briefing to Senate Armed Services Committee, 4-5.

[33] Shine, 27.

[34] Centers for Disease Control and Prevention, 4-12.

[35] Budgetary analysis from Bolton, 4, and C. Stephen Redhead, et al., "Bioterrorism: Legislation to Improve Public Health Preparedness and Response Capability, Updated May 8, 2002", Congressional Research Service (Washington, D.C. Library of Congress, 2002) 2-33, and Tommy Thompson, "Bioterrorism." Testimony before Senate Appropriations Committee, 2 May 2002, available from <http://www.hhs.gov/news/speech/2002/020502.html>; Internet; accessed 21 September 2002.

[36] "A Homeland Security Plan." New Democrats Online 15 November 2001[journal on-line]; available from <http://www.ndol.org/ndol ci.cfm?contentid=250723&kaid=139&subid=271>; Internet; accessed 21 September 2002, 1.

[37] Roberts, 1.

[38] This new doctrine on deterrence and dissuasion is a compilation from several sources. The most coherent discussion on the new doctrine is found in Michael J Powers, Deterring Terrorism With CBRN Weapons: Developing a Conceptual Framework (Washington, D.C.: Chemical and Biological Arms Control Institute, February 2001), 1-10.

[39] Thompson speech to National Governors Association.

[40] Range, 2-3.

[41] Thompson speech to National Governors Association.

[42] Centers for Disease Control and Prevention, 6-10.

[43] These recommendations are a compilation of recommendations from various sources, including Third Annual Report to the President and Congress of the Advisory Panel to Assess Domestic Response Capabilities for Terrorism Involving Weapons of Mass Destruction (Arlington: RAND Corporation, 15 December 2001), and Roberts, 1-8., and National Strategy for Homeland Security, 1-30.

[44] Roberts, 7.

[45] Range, 2.

[46] "A Homeland Security Plan.", 1-2, and Strongin, 4.

[47] Range, 2.

[48] For an excellent discussion of further recommendations for strengthening the Biologic Weapons Convention, please see Christian Enemark, Protection Pending: Changing the Lock on Pandora's Box, (Champaign: ACDIS, 2000), 11-19.

[49] There are several articles that discuss the possible impact of The Model State Emergency Health Powers Act. Please see James C. Hodge, Jr., "Bioterrorism law and policy: Critical choices in public health," The Journal of Law, Medicine and Ethics, 30, no.2 (Summer 2002), 254-261 [database on-line]; available from ProQuest; accessed 13 December 2002; Andrew Goldstein, "Mr. Quarantine, meet Miss Liberty," Time, 159, no.14 (8 April 2002), 19 [database on-line]; available from ProQuest; accessed 13 December 2002; and Thomas W. Washburne, "Review of the Model State Emergency Health Powers Act," 20 December 2001; available from <http://www.hslda.org/docs/nche/000010/200112201.asp>; Internet; accessed 13 December 2002.

[50] Centers for Disease Control and Prevention, 13.

BIBLIOGRAPHY

"A Homeland Security Plan." New Democrats Online 15 November 2001. Journal on-line. Available from <http://www.ndol.org/ndol_ci.cfm?contentid=250723&kaid=139 &subid=271>.Internet. Accessed 21 September 2002.

Bush, George W. The National Security Strategy of the United States of America Washington, D.C.: The White House, September 2002.

Bush, George W. National Strategy for Homeland Security. Washington, D.C.: Office Of Homeland Security, July 2002.

Butler, Jay C. et al. "Collaboration Between Public Health and Law Enforcement: New Paradigms and Partnerships for Bioterrorism Planning and Response." Emerging Infectious Diseases 10 (October 2002): 1-9.

Carus, W. Seth. Working Paper Bioterrorism and Biocrimes. Washington, D.C.: Center For Counterproliferation Research, National Defense University, August 1998 (February 2001 Revision).

Center for Counterproliferation Research. Chemical, Biological, Radiological, and Nuclear Terrorism: The Threat According to the Current Unclassified Literature. Washington, D.C.: National Defense University, 31 May 2002.

Centers for Disease Control and Prevention. " Biological and Chemical Terrorism: Strategic Plan for Preparedness and Response. Recommendations of the CDC Strategic Planning Workgroup." Morbidity and Mortality Weekly Report 49(No.RR-4) (2000): 1-14.

Cilifullo, Frank J., Sharon L. Cardash, and Gordon N Lederman. Combating Chemical, Biological, Radiological and Nuclear Terrorism: A Comprehensive Strategy. Washington, D.C.: Center for Strategic and International Studies, December 2000.

Cilifullo, Frank J. et al. Defending America in the 21st Century New Challenges, New Organizations, and New Policies. Washington, D.C.: Center for Strategic and International Studies, 2000.

Dando, Malcolm. Biologic Warfare in the 21st Century. New York: Brassey's, 1994.

_____. The New Biological Weapons Threat, Proliferation, and Control Boulder: Lynne Rienner, 2001.

Daniels, Anthony. "Germs Against Man." National Review 53 (3 December 2001): 42-44.

Drell, Sidney et al., eds. The New Terror Facing the Threat of Biological and Chemical Weapons. Stanford: Hoover Institute Press/Stanford University, 1999.

Eisenstein, Maurice, and Brian K. Houghton, eds. Bioterrorism: Homeland Defense; An Executive Summary of the Rand Symposium. Santa Monica: RAND Corporation, October 2000.

Enemark, Christian. Protection Pending: Changing the Lock on Pandora's Box. Champaign: ACDIS, 2000.

Federal Emergency Management Agency. Federal Response Plan, Terrorism Incident Annex. Washington, D.C.: U.S. Printing Office, April 1999, TI1-16.

Frist, Bill. When Every Moment Counts. Boulder: Rowman & Littlefield, 2002.

General Accounting Office. Bioterrorism Federal Research and Preparedness Activities. Washington, D.C.: US General Accounting Office, September 2001.

Giblin, James Cross. When Plague Strikes: The Black Death, Smallpox, AIDS. New York: HarperCollins, 1995.

Goldstein, Andrew. "Mr. Quarantine, meet Miss Liberty." 159 no.14 (8 April 2002): 19. Database on-line. Available from ProQuest. Accessed 13 December 2002.

Health and Human Services Fact Sheet. "17 Critical Benchmarks for Bioterrorism Preparedness Planning." 6 June 2002. Available from <http://www.hhs.gov/news/press/2002press/ 20020606.html>. Internet. Accessed 21 September 2002.

Hodge, James C. Jr. "Bioterrorism law and policy: Critical choices in public health." 30 no. 2 (Summer 2002): 254-261. Database on-line. Available from ProQuest. Accessed 13 December 2002.

Jane's Chemical-Biological Defense Guidebook. 15 April 2000. Database on-line. Available from ProQuest. Accessed 21 September 2002.

Kearney, Bill. "Better Plan Needed to protect U.S. Agriculture From Bioterror Attack." News of the National Academies 19 September 2002. Journal on-line. Available from <http://www4.nationalacademies.org/news.nsf/isbn/0309085454?OpenDocument>. Internet. Accessed 21 September 2002.

Miller, Judith et al. Germs Biologic Weapons and America's Secret War. New York: Simon & Schuster, 2001.

The Model State Emergency Health Powers Act (Draft as of 23 October 2001). Washington, D.C.: Center for Law and the Public's Health at Georgetown and Johns Hopkins Universities, 2001.

Morse, Stephen. "The Vigilance Defense." Scientific American 287 (October 2002) 4, 88-9.

Parker, Henry S. Agricultural Bioterrorism: A Federal Strategy to Meet the Threat. Washington, D.C.: Institute for National Strategic Studies, National Defense University, 2002.

Powers, Michael J. Deterring Terrorism With CBRN Weapons: Developing a Conceptual Framework. Washington, D.C.: Chemical and Biological Arms Control Institute, February 2001.

Public Health Security and Bioterrorism Preparedness and Response Act of 2002. House
Resolution 3448, 107th Cong., 2nd sess., 23 January 2002.

Range, Peter Ross. "Preparing for Bioterrorism." New Democrats Online. 15 November 2001.
Journal on-line. Available from <http://www.ndol.org/ndol_ci.cfm?contentid=3924
&kaid=124&subid=160>.Internet. Accessed 21 September 2002.

Redhead, C. Stephen et al. "Bioterrorism: Legislation to Improve Public Health Preparedness and
Response Capability, Updated May 8, 2002." Congressional Research Service, Library of
Congress, Washington, DC.

Roberts, Brad and Michael Moodie. "Biologic Weapons: Toward a Threat Reduction Strategy."
Defense Horizons 15 (July 2002): 1-8.

Shine, Kenneth. "Bioterrorism From Panic to Preparedness." RAND Review August 2002. Journal
on-line. Available from <http://www.rand.org/publications/randreview/issues/
rr.08.02/bioterrorism.html>. Internet. Accessed 21 September 2002.

Smithson, Amy and Leslie Ann Levy. Ataxia: The Chemical and Biological Terrorism Threat and
US Response. Washington, D.C.: The Henry L. Stimson Center, 1999.

Strongin, Robin J. ed. Emergency Preparedness from a Health Perspective: Preparing for
Bioterrorism at the Federal, State and Local Levels. Washington, D.C.: National Health
Policy Forums, George Washington University, October 2001.

Third Annual Report to the President and Congress of the Advisory Panel to Assess Domestic
Response Capabilities for Terrorism Involving Weapons of Mass Destruction. Arlington:
RAND Corporation, 15 December 2001.

Thompson, Tommy. "Bioterrorism." Testimony before Senate Appropriations Committee,
Washington, DC. 2 May 2002. Available from <http://www.hhs.gov/news/speech/2002/
020502.html>. Internet. Accessed 21 September 2002.

Thompson, Tommy. "Facing the Threat of Bioterrorism: Plans and Priorities for the Bush
Administration." Speech given to the National Governors Association, 10 July 2001.
Available from <http://www.hhs.gov/news/speech/2001/010710.html>. Internet. Accessed
21 September 2002.

Uniting and Strengthening America by Providing Appropriate Tools Required to Intercept and
Obstruct Terrorism (USA Patriot Act) Act of 2001. HR 3162, 107th Cong., 1st sess., 24
October 2001.

U.S. Congress. Senate. Armed Services Committee. Subcommittee on National Security.
Combating Terrorism: Federal Response to a Biologic Weapons Attack. 107th Cong., 1st
sess., 23 July 2001.

Washburne, Thomas W. "Review of the Model State Emergency Health Powers Act." 20
December 2001. Available from <http://www.hslda.org/docs/nche/000010/
200112201.asp>. Internet. Accessed 13 December 2002.